Inspired

Sam Daniels

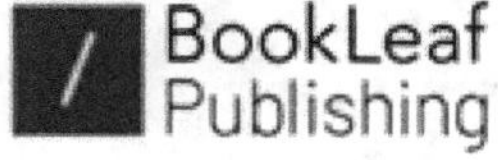

Presentation by *BookLeaf Publishing*

Web: www.bookleafpub.com

E-mail: info@bookleafpub.com

ISBN: 9789357210485

First edition 2022

DEDICATION

In Loving memory of a Special little boy, who was taken far to soon. X

ACKNOWLEDGEMENT

Thankyou to my mum for supporting me through this. Also for your help with writing some of the poems within.

Charlie Bear 1

There is not a Bear like Charlie Bear.
 As Charlie Bears are rare,
Charlie Bear is a brave Bear.
 And Charlie Bear does care.
Charlie Bear is happy Bear,
A kind and loving sole.
Charlie Bear is special Bear,
 He is one of the Best.
Charlie Bear is right up there,
 He puts you to the test.
Charlie Bear likes music.
 Lights and lots of fun,
Charlie Bear is the only Bear,
 As he is my number one.

River

The river flows through a wooded glade,
rippling gently as it goes.
Flowers nod gently with the breeze, while it
gently passes with ease.
Kingfishers fish, as the river flows, Sitting on
branches above the water.
The birds flying high while the river makes it
way; the sun beating down
On the dense woodland floor.
While Squirrels and Rabbits scuttle around on
the wild bank of the river.
Busy going about their daily lives.
Watching the river as it passes on by.

My Guardian Angel

My Guardian Angel, what a precious thing?
You came into my life like a snowdrop in spring.
You had so many issues, but you battled on
through.
A warrior like no other, that was you.
Through the good and bad times, you sparkled
like glitter.
You made everything possible, and life not so
bitter.

I promised too always be there, and that I always
would be.
I cannot be with you now, but your still part of
me.
I cannot cuddle you or read you a story.
But I have precious memories and have you as
my story.
My Guardian Angel, which is what you will
always be,
Shining so bright but watching over me.

Charlie Bear 2

Charlie Bear is a special Bear.
And Charlie Bear is fine,
Charlie Bear is a loving bear,
As Charlie Bear is mine.

Charlie bear, is a mischievous Bear,
He will have you on the run.
Charlie Bear is a happy bear,
Who loves lots of fun?

Charlie Bear, cannot walk or talk,
But that does not stop him at all.
Charlie Bear, is a brave bear,
He has been through it all.

Charlie Bear is a clever bear,
You meet him and you will see.
Charlie Bear is a unique Bear,
Who belongs to me?

We all have our favourite Bears.
But Charlie Bear is mine,
Charlie Bear is a special Bear
And Charlie Bear is fine.

I Love you Charlie Bear
From the bottom of my heart.

Sunrise over the Mountains

The early morning sunrise over the mountain gleams.
Shinning brightly flowing down streams,
Radiating softly over valleys and hills.
Lighting up grasslands, bouncing off rocks and trees.
Birds swiftly swooping, riding the thermals feeling the breeze.
Sun Rising brightly high in the sky,
Reaching as far as the land doth lie.
Mountains standing firm and strong,
While life all around carries on.

Percy

I call him Percy, he sits on my wall.
He isn't very large, but not really small,
I saw him first as i was dusting.
He seemed so cute, and very trusting.
So i leave him be, he deals with the flies. I like
my spider, hes got cute eyes.
I hope he stays, hes my little pet.
At least with a spider you don't need a vet.

Charlie Bear 3

Charlie bear is a special Bear,
And Charlie Bear is Kind
Charlie Bear is special Bear,
As Charlie Bear is mine.
Charlie Bear, was a character,
He was always very bright.
Charlie Bear, You cuddled me
Each and every night.

Charlie Bear you loved Mozart,
And Winnie the Pooh.
Mummy is so very lucky.
To have had a Charlie Bear like you.

Charlie bear you loved,
The Greatest Showman
 the song "this is me".
Charlie Bear you were good,
And never did any wrong.

Charlie bear you were my warrior,
Brave and really strong.
You made people smile
A hero to so many,
Yet only met by a few.

Charlie Bear your kisses,
Well, they were simply the best.
Your snuggles were great too,
Charlie Bear you were impressive
I adore you!

Charlie Bear your special
And Charlie Bear your fine,
Charlie Bears live forever.
And I'm lucky, as you were mine.

Waterfall

Over the Waterfall, it crashes
The whiteness of the water as it foams below.
Splashing on the rocks and spraying a fine mist
in the air.
The blue sky above, birds circling over head.
Bears fishing at the waters edge playing as they
go.
The clear water shows the fish, who are trying to
hide below.

Best Friends

Hooligan-Annie was always there for you.
She was your best friend, mine too.
She used to walk with me, before you even
arrived.
If we said we could not take her, she cried.
She protected you from social workers,
And anybody new, she knew how to care for
you.
She knew exactly what to do.
She wrapped herself around you,
In your car seat, she knew you were vulnerable,
Her love you could not beat.
She would get between those, of which she did
not trust.
She was always protecting you, that was her
must.

She knew that you were poorly and at my belly
sat,
She knew you had not come home.
I could not argue with that.
She loved to give you kisses and check that you
were okay.
She stayed your best friend, till her dying day.

You could not have had a better friend and
Hooligan Annie was she,
I miss her and you combined, but best friends
you will always be.

Growing Fondly in my heart

You grow so fondly in my heart,
My memories of you bloom.
You have become, my Guardian Angel,
You were taken far too soon.

You grow to be a shining star.
And bloom, like a daffodil in spring,
You become to mean so much more.
That I cherish everything.

Smiling Brightly

I am wrapped up in your snuggles,
Your smiles shine like stars.
Your Cheeky personality is forever ours.

You bought a lot of joy to us,
And we shed so many tears.
But your smile lives on Forever,
And will do so for years.

You are in my heart,
And that is where you will stay.
My Cheeky little Monkey,
Who's smile made my day.

Autumn

Walking past a hedgerow,
Listening to the Rustle.
Hear the birds a chirping,
The Hustle and Bustle.

The leaves as they change colour,
The flowers not in bloom.
The bracken in the flower bed,
The cloudy sky at noon.

Walking past the hedgerow,
The dew coming from the leaves.
The grass all white with frost,
The cold wintery Breeze.

The autumnal feeling within,
 How much I love the autumn,
And the changes that it will bring.

Your special day

On your special day, we gathered to say
goodbye.
You are being the little star, which will forever
shine so high.
Your teddies cuddled up to you,
Blankets to keep you warm.
All your favourite people,
Who came to say goodbye?
Dressed up just for you, as a unicorn,
Winnie the Pooh, or Elf.
Reading the Wonky Donkey,
A book off mummy's shelf.

Lots of Beautiful songs,
Lights and Colour, just for you.
So many things, that will never get to do.
I miss you every day, I did not really say
Goodbye.
To me, My cheeky monkey,
You did not really die.

A new Beginning

A new beginning sometimes it's what we need.
Something different, someplace new.
I really don't know what, I actually could do.
I want to move, but comfortable in this place.
Does this frustration show on my face?
A new beginning, but where and when?
I don't know now and I didn't know then.
Time to start over, but its so hard to do,
how do I live in a world without you.

On a dessert Island

I'm laying on a dessert Island, the sun is
beaming down.
Sitting on the sand, with sea all around.
The palm trees high above, so incredibly tall
Coconuts ready to fall.
The golden sands softly round my feet,
The sun on my back and I'm feeling the heat.
Time to get up and paddle, at the waters edge.
So refreshing and calm.
So I'm on a dessert island and
everything is fine.
I'm on a dessert island and it's mine.

Charlie Bear 4

Charlie Bear is going to Demelza.
As Charlie Bear is poorly,
So Charlie Bear can have a rest
And get special care as well.

Charlie Bear loves the carers
 And they love Charlie Bear too.
So today they're doing painting,
Let's see what else they do.

Charlie Bears feet are painted blue.
Oh, so bright! they add on twinkly stars,
 So it glows up late at night.

Charlie bear has had an exciting day
 And has watched some Winnie the pooh.
Now Charlie Bear is listening to music,
Then what's he going to do?.

The carers are changing over
And Charlie Bear is going to bed.
 The carers turn out the twinkly lights,
So Charlie Bear can rest his head.

We Love you Charlie Bear,
Sleep tight my special one.
Demelza is an awesome place,
For poorly bears to have some fun.

Stars

The sunshine's wherever you are.
The sky so rich and blue.
When the stars come out at night,
They remind me of you.

They sparkle high above,
And shine so bright and true,
When the sun is shining,
It warms my heart,
I Know we aren't apart.

The sun shines like stars;
And then they fade away,
But your always here,
Sparkling everyday.

Time Passes

Time does not alleviate, the sorrow of grief,
It cannot be healed and gives no relief.
Like procrastination it is a thief.

Locked inside is so much pain,
Which cannot be altered or washed with rain.

It is a feeling that is impossible to explain.

Like flower petals that have long since died,
All I feel is an emptiness inside.
Although my heartbreaks, like waves on the
shore.
The pain of grief is so incredibly raw.